INSIDE CRIME

INSIDE CRIME

GUN CRIME

by Dirk Flint

Smart Apple Media

Published by Smart Apple Media
P.O. Box 3263, Mankato, Minnesota 56002

Printed in the United States of America at Corporate Graphics, in North Mankato, Minnesota.

Published by arrangement with the Watts Publishing Group LTD, London.

Library of Congress Cataloging-in-Publication Data

Flint, Dirk.
Gun crime / by Dirk Flint.
p. cm.—(Inside crime)
Includes index.
Summary: "Gives information on various types of gun crimes and discusses the laws of different countries and their attitude toward guns. Includes real-life examples and case studies of gun crimes around the world"—Provided by publisher.
ISBN 978-1-59920-395-9 (library binding)
1. Gun control—Juvenile literature. 2. Violent crime—Juvenile literature. 3. Firearms ownership—Juvenile literature. I. Title.
HV7435.F575 2012
364.15—dc22

2010046771

1306
3-2011

9 8 7 6 5 4 3 2 1

Series editor: Jeremy Smith
Editors: Julia Bird
Design: sprout.uk.com
Artworks: sprout.uk.com
Picture researcher: Diana Morris

Picture credits: Ace Stock Ltd/Alamy: front cover b. Action Press/Rex Features: 16. Allstar PL/Alamy: 39b. AP/PAI: 10, 11. Austral Int/Rex Features: 40. Julien Behal/PA Wire/PAI: 14.Bettmann/Corbis: 8. Ashley Cooper/Alamy: 28. Anthony Devlin/PA Wire/PAI: 15tr. Bill Gadbury /Shutterstock: 15tl. Getty Images: 36. Greg Goodman/Shutterstock: front cover t. Johnny Green/PA Archive/PAI: 37. Themba Hadebe/AP/PAI: 24. haveseen/Shutterstock: front cover c, 5. KPA/Zuma/Rex Features: 35. Jose Luis Magana/AP/PAI: 27t. John McLellan/Rex Features: 21. Met Police/AP/Topfoto: 29. Kevin Moroney/Aurora Photos/Alamy: 13b. Martin Moxter/Imagebroker/Alamy: 39t. National Pictures/Topfoto: 30, 41. NewsPictures/MCP/Rex Features: 12. OJO Images/Rex Features: 9. PA/PAI: 22br. Photos 12/Alamy: 38. Rex Features: 17, 25, 27b. Martin Smith-Rodden/AP/PAI: 33. Thomas Sbampato/Imagebroker/Alamy: 19. Martin H Simon/Corbis: 32. Sipa Press/Rex Features: 18, 23, 26, 31. Steve Starr/Corbis: 34. Mark St George/Rex Features: 22bl. Jason Stitt/istockphoto: 13t. Mark J Terrill/AP/PAI: 20.

INSIDE CRIME INS

CONTENTS

GUN CRIME— OUT OF CONTROL?

In many parts of the world, violent crime is on the rise. Read the papers, and barely a week goes by when there isn't a headline about a gang shooting, armed robbery, or the seizure of illegal guns by police officers or customs officials. Can anything be done to control such gun crime, and should there be tougher laws about owning a gun?

The Right to Bear Arms

In the United States, the debate about gun ownership has gone on for hundreds of years. In 1791, the Bill of Rights declared the "right of the people to keep and bear arms," and when the state of Georgia tried to ban handguns in 1837, the law was thrown out. In the late 1930s, the United States passed laws requiring gun owners to have a licence and banning the sale of weapons to convicted criminals. These laws were poorly enforced, however, and it was only after the shooting of President John F. Kennedy in 1963 that the United States clamped down on sales of firearms.

▼ *President John F. Kennedy rides with his wife Jacqueline in a motorcade in Dallas, Texas, on November 22, 1963. Moments later, Kennedy was shot by an assassin. Kennedy is one of four U.S. presidents to be assassinated by gunmen.*

Fewer Guns, Fewer Deaths?

Despite tighter controls on the sale of weapons, the argument continues to rage over the link between guns and violent crimes such as murder and armed robbery. One view is that the high murder rate in the United States is a direct result of the fact that so many Americans own firearms. If there were fewer guns, there would be fewer deaths. Others argue that guns can protect innocent people from violence and actually prevent crime: if a robber walks into a shop and the owner takes out a weapon, the robber will think twice about committing a crime.

▲ *It is sometimes said that guns don't kill, people do. However, there is an undeniable link between gun ownership and deaths caused by shooting.*

Around the World

While the problem of gun crime is bad in the United States, it is even more of an issue in some South American countries where it is linked to the powerful and lucrative drug trade. Gun deaths are also on the rise in countries such as Russia, Ireland, and Australia.

WHAT IS GUN CRIME?

Gun crime is any crime carried out with a firearm. Gun crimes are serious because guns kill. Victims of assaults with a knife are five times less likely to die than shooting victims. Even if robbers do not intend to harm their victims, a bank robbery can turn into a fatal shooting if they panic and fire.

The Rise of Gun Violence

Although pistols were invented in the 16th century, guns weren't used much until the 20th century. In 1900, the U.S. murder rate was about one per 100,000 people, compared to a high of about 20 in the 1980s. One reason is that people weren't used to handling guns until World War I (1914–1918), when millions were drafted into the army. The introduction of mass production also meant that guns were more readily available in the 20th century. The 1920s saw the dramatic use of machine guns by mobsters in cities such as Chicago, and the majority of gun crime today is still linked to criminal gangs.

Deliberate or Accidental?

Some gun crimes are deliberate. But guns can also lead to unplanned deaths. These types of shootings often involve people who know each other. In the heat of an argument, one may pull out a gun and finish the fight. A husband may kill his wife in this way, or a young man may kill a friend or parent. Children who come across a weapon in the house may fire it accidentally.

► Legendary gangster Al Capone lived by the gun. The Chicago mobster was probably behind the Saint Valentine's Day Massacre on February 14, 1929, when seven men were brutally gunned down in a Chicago garage.

▲ *Police investigate a shooting in the Mexican border town of Ciudad Juárez. The city is a major battle ground for drug cartels, and 5,000 people have been murdered there since 2006, earning it the name of "the most violent city on Earth."*

Some gun violence statistics include self-inflicted injuries—suicide victims often use a gun. Suicides account for almost half of the 30,000 gun deaths in the United States each year, while accidental gun deaths account for another 700.

Lethal Weapon

Because guns are so deadly, the police take gun crimes very seriously. In the United States, gun crime is seen as one of the most troubling types of criminal activity. Yet gun crime in the U.S. is actually less than that in countries like Colombia and Mexico, where an all-out war between the police and rival drug gangs has led to a string of bloody gunfights and brutal murders, along with a rash of gun factory raids and smuggling busts.

FACT FILE

Gun crime is often linked to poverty. Most studies reveal you are more likely to be shot in a deprived neighborhood. However, crime has many causes, including culture. Japan has a very low rate of gun crime: in 2006 there were just 53 shootings in a population of over 127 million. Japan has tight gun controls, but the low gun crime rate is probably due to the fact that in Japanese culture, it is very important to conform and respect your fellow citizens.

WHAT GUNS ARE USED?

Since the 1960s, the kinds of weapons used in murders and violent crime haven't changed all that much. While rifles and shotguns account for 15 percent of all homicides, more than half of all murders are carried out with handguns, probably due to the fact that they are easier to conceal and buy illegally. As a result, most countries have stricter laws controlling handguns.

Criminals and Guns

All guns use gunpowder to blast a bullet out of a barrel at high speed and with deadly force. The most lethal are automatic weapons and machine guns that can hold and fire a large number of rounds (bullets) very quickly. Criminal gangs in many countries now use weapons like these in battles with rival gangs and the police. Other long-barreled weapons include shotguns, which are devastating at close range. Criminals often saw off part of the barrel to make them easier to carry and conceal. Hunting rifles can fire a single shot accurately over a long distance. They are typically used by assassins and serial killers rather than in street crimes.

▼ Two armed gang members are at a drug selling point in Rio de Janeiro, Brazil. The man on the left is carrying an automatic rifle. This deadly weapon is capable of firing many bullets in quick succession.

◄ *Handguns such as this pistol are a favorite among street gangs, as they are cheap, simple to use, and easily hidden.*

Semiautomatics

Automatic weapons and shotguns may be more deadly, but street criminals, especially young gang members, often prefer semiautomatic pistols because of their look and the fact that they can hold 10 or more rounds. Because of their size, these pistols are also easy to hide. The cheapest can be bought for $100 or even less.

Heavy Weapons

Some terrorist groups set out to kill as many people as possible, so they are more likely to be armed with heavy weapons such as assault rifles, rocket launchers, and heavy machine guns. In the past, terrorists have also used special weapons such as the Glock plastic gun, which could pass through a metal detector. However, since the 2001 attacks on the World Trade Center and the Pentagon, there has been much tighter security at airports.

▼ *Most guns are made of metal and show up on the X-ray machines and metal detectors used by airport security.*

ON TARGET

United States firearms laws vary from state to state, but some federal agencies and laws govern them, too. The federal Bureau of Alcohol, Tobacco, Firearms, and Explosives (ATF), regulates gun licensing. Laws, such as the Gun Control Act of 1968 and the Brady Handgun Violence Prevention Act of 1993, restrict the sale of guns between states and require a federal background check for people who purchase guns.

WHO COMMITS GUN CRIMES?

Many people who carry guns set out to kill or hurt others, such as a paid assassin or hitmen working for a drug gang. Guns are also weapons of terror. Kidnappers and robbers use them to scare other people into handing over money or valuables. The danger is that as violent crime increases, more people will also buy guns to protect themselves, leading to more accidental shootings and deaths.

▲ *Kidnappers and other criminals use guns to intimidate their victims and keep them under control.*

Why Carry a Gun?

A gun offers criminals several advantages over weapons such as knives. With a gun in their hand, robbers can keep their distance, making it easier to make a getaway and harder for a victim to fight back. Guns also give criminals a psychological advantage. It's much easier to control a bank full of staff, for example, with a gun than with a knife. For others, guns are a form of protection and security. Whatever the reason, if someone can get their hands on a gun when they lose their temper or panic, they're far more likely to kill someone else.

Men and Guns

Some people, more often men, become obsessed with guns. Some are just enthusiasts who enjoy polishing their weapons, firing them at a shooting range, or hunting. Other men like the feeling of power a gun gives them. Some experts say hormones such as testosterone make men naturally more aggressive.

◀ *Many young boys enjoy playing with toy or replica guns.*

Others argue that boys are often taught to be tough or aggressive. Whatever the reason, men are usually the ones who use guns. Worldwide, around 90 percent of all robberies and violent attacks are carried out by men.

Gang Violence

In many countries, criminal gangs are responsible for the majority of gun crime. A small incident can quickly lead to all-out war. A bloody battle between Jamaican gangs broke out after a pair of sunglasses was stolen. A deadly gang feud in the city of Limerick, Ireland, started in the early 2000s after a fight in a school playground resulted in a schoolgirl getting her face slashed. The violence quickly escalated, and in November 2000, gunmen pumped a rival gang member full of bullets in a crowded bar. Since then, there have been over 15 gun deaths linked to the feud.

ON TARGET

There is a growing trend in the United States and Europe for teenage girls to get dragged into the gun culture by hiding weapons for their criminal boyfriends or relatives. In the United Kingdom, for example, the trend was concerning enough for police to launch a TV campaign in 2009 targeting young women. The campaign, which used the tagline "Hide his gun and you help commit the crime," let women know that they could go to prison for storing weapons. In one instance, police found a 16-year-old with a loaded pistol in her bedroom.

▶ *Though most armed criminals are men, female friends and relatives can get caught up in violent crime by hiding their weapons for them.*

CASE STUDY: KILLING SPREES

Some kinds of gun crime are particularly hard for the police to combat. Mass murderers can go on a killing "spree" with little or no warning, and several gun massacres have been carried out by teenagers with no previous criminal record.

Student Massacres

Gun massacres have taken place in many parts of the world, but they are particularly common in schools and colleges. On August 1, 1966, Charles Joseph Whitman, a student at the University of Texas in Austin, killed 14 people and wounded 32 at the university campus in the first known killing spree of its kind. Around the world, on March 11, 2009 17-year-old Tim Kretschmer went on a shooting spree at his old school in Winnenden, Germany, and at a local car dealership. He killed 16 people before turning the gun on himself.

Columbine

Perhaps the most notorious school massacre took place in 1999, when two students, 18-year-old Dylan Klebold and 17-year-old Eric Harris, went on a rampage at Columbine High School in Littleton, Colorado. In the months before the massacre, they had managed to buy two handguns, two shotguns, and a semiautomatic rifle, as well as ammunition and explosives.

▼ *Local residents leave floral tributes near the school in Winnenden, Germany, where Tim Kretschmer killed nine students and one teacher.*

On the morning of April 20, Klebold and Harris planted bombs hidden inside duffel bags in the school cafeteria. They went back to their cars, but when the bombs failed to explode, they armed themselves and walked back to the school. In just 15 minutes, they shot and killed 12 students and a teacher, and they injured another 21 students before killing themselves.

Because the two shooters committed suicide, it was hard to know what their motives were and whether anything could have been done to stop them. A report by the FBI argued that both students had mental health problems. Other experts blamed video games and movies or debated whether Klebold and Harris were bullied at school.

ON TARGET

What can be done to prevent school massacres?

- Most attacks happen so quickly that armed police only arrive after the shooter has finished. That said, police departments in some countries are now trained to stop the shooter at all costs, to prevent him from killing more.
- In the United States, many university campuses now have electronic devices that can lock doors or send emergency e-mails and phone messages. Many schools have evacuation drills in case of an emergency.
- Some colleges have programs that try to identify and provide treatment for students who might pose a risk. However, a U.S. Secret Service study showed that shooters come from many different backgrounds. Most were not misfits and had no history of violence.
- More controversial are calls that students should be allowed to carry guns so that they can protect themselves. Many worry this could lead to accidental deaths.

▼ Eric Harris and Dylan Klebold were caught on CCTV in the cafeteria during their killing spree at Columbine High School on April 20, 1999. One of the most frightening aspects of the tragedy was how easily the pair obtained firearms.

HOW MUCH GUN CRIME IS THERE?

The amount of gun crime can vary a great deal from country to country. It is particularly high in places where organized crime or drug gangs are very powerful (see page 11). Gun crime is also more common in countries such as South Africa where there is a big divide between rich and poor. Almost everywhere, violent crime is higher in big cities, as this is where gangs are usually based.

▲ *The police in countries such as Colombia, where drug-related killings are a big problem, have to be extra vigilant. Here, Colombian police are checking bus passengers at a roadblock for weapons and drugs.*

Low Levels in Europe

In most developed countries in Europe, the overall level of gun crime is generally very low. For example, over the last 10 years, between 40 and 100 people have been killed each year by firearms in the UK, with around 20,000 incidents each year involving guns. While very frightening for the victims, most did not result in injury. In fact, in recent years, four times more people were killed by knives than by guns in the United Kingdom. This may be due in part to the UK's strict laws on gun ownership, as few ordinary citizens have access to guns.

A Gun Culture?

In contrast, gun crime is high in the United States, where a quarter of robberies are carried out with guns. Here around 12,000 people are shot every year—accounting for more than two out of every three killings. That's an average of 33 people every day.

Some blame the gun culture in the United States, where it is relatively easy to buy a gun. In most U.S. states, as long as you are 21 and have no criminal record, you simply need a driver's licence or some other form of ID to buy a pistol legally. John Hinkley, the man who tried to kill President Ronald Reagan, used forged ID papers and paid only $27 for the gun he used. Around 40 percent of American households own a gun, usually for self-defense. Unfortunately, this leads to around 700 to 800 accidental deaths each year.

▼ Many U.S. citizens defend their right to carry weapons, especially in wilderness areas such as Alaska where hunting is popular. Problems arise when these guns get into the hands of children or people with mental health problems.

BUSTED!

One of the arguments in favor of owning guns in the United States is the fact that firearms can be used in self-defense or to stop a crime. In January 2002, for example, two students at the Appalachian School of Law in Virginia ran to their cars and took out pistols after hearing gunfire. They used them to disarm a shooter who had already killed three people, including the dean of the school, and wounded three more. Some have used the case to call for people at educational institutions to be allowed to arm themselves.

GETTING HOLD OF GUNS

A determined criminal usually has no problem getting hold of a gun. In the United States, guns are freely available at gun shows, pawn shops, and flea markets. In European countries, firearms are smuggled in from countries with more relaxed gun laws and sold on the black market or the Internet. If all else fails, weapons can be stolen—around 500,000 guns are stolen every year in the United States.

◄ *Although local authorities often try to ban gun shows such as this one in Pomona, California, they remain extremely popular.*

Freely Available

It can be very hard for the police to stop criminals getting guns. Seung-Hui Cho, a student who went on an armed rampage at Virginia Tech in April 2007, simply ordered a gun on the Internet and picked it up from a local pawn shop. Although pistols, shotguns, and rifles can be bought legally from stores in the United States, criminals prefer to buy weapons on the black market so they are harder to trace. For example, a popular gang weapon is the Russian SKS assault rifle. Even a very powerful weapon like this may only cost about $100. Gun traffickers like to peddle handguns because they can buy them at such rock-bottom prices. Then they can tack on a hefty mark-up and still sell them cheaply to gang members.

Drugs and Guns

The trade in guns is often linked to other crimes. Drug addicts who break into homes can trade stolen guns for drugs, for example. The drug dealer then sells the guns to criminals such as carjackers and robbers. Though firearms manufacturers are required by law to put serial numbers on guns, it is very hard to track a gun once it has entered this second-hand market.

BUSTED!

For some, dealing in death is a highly profitable business. Former British soldier Paul Alexander ran a secret gun factory and supplied feuding gangs with assassination kits and other weapons, which were linked to a murder, four attempted murders, and an armed robbery. Each kit cost $2,400 and contained a handgun, silencer, and three or four magazines with up to 11 rounds in them. The police finally closed in on Alexander after his DNA was discovered on a handgun seized two years before. The barn where he worked contained 12,000 gun parts and 28 guns and rifles.

▼ *Former army sergeant Paul Alexander, shown here in police custody, supplied weapons to criminal gangs that were linked to 28 firearms crimes in the United Kingdom.*

CONTROLS AND PENALTIES

Guns make it easy to kill, so in most developed countries there are strict controls on owning or buying a gun. In the United States, certain people are ineligible to have a gun license, and only licensed dealers can sell guns across state lines. However, gun control laws differ widely from one country to another. Despite the various arguments, countries with fewer guns do tend to have fewer gun crimes.

Self-Defense

In the United States, gun rights groups argue that people have a right to defend themselves. In Britain, a person may use "reasonable force" to protect themselves or others or to prevent a crime. But what is reasonable force? In the United States, a person can shoot an intruder if his or her life is threatened. This is known as justifiable homicide, and the person who shoots an intruder is not charged with any crime.

In Britain, people have been sent to jail for shooting intruders. The most well known case is Tony Martin. In 1999, this farmer shot and killed an intruder in his home. He was sentenced to life in prison, but after an appeal his sentence was reduced to three years.

For and Against

Gun rights groups claim that guns kept in a house can often be used to scare a robber or intruder away without needing to fire a shot. On the other hand, those in favor of gun control point to the fact that a gun in a home is far more likely to result in injury or death for someone living there. The spread of guns also breeds fear. In a survey carried out in 2005, almost 40 percent of the U.S. teenagers interviewed believed they would be shot at some point in their lives, and the same percentage felt gun violence could break out in their school.

▼ *British farmer Tony Martin (left) became the focus of a huge debate in the United Kingdom after killing a teenager who broke into his home and wounding another, Brendan Fearon (right).*

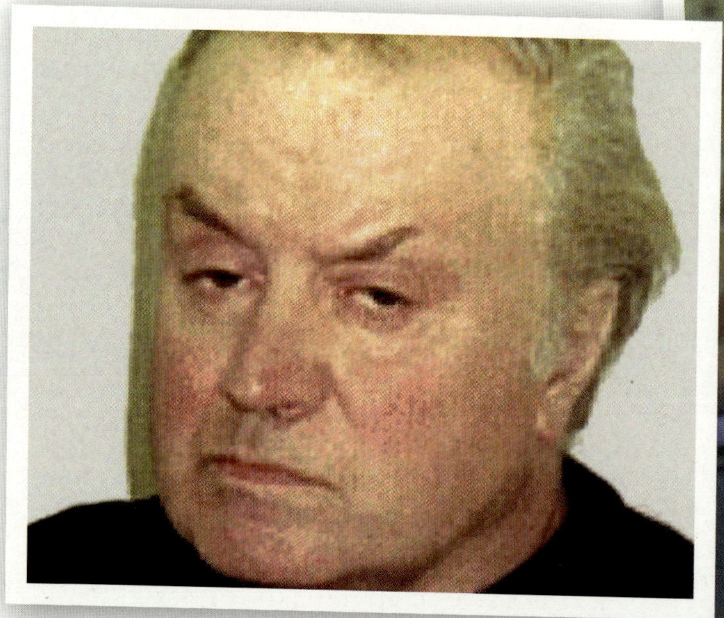

▲ *Though China's weapon laws are very strict, gun crime is still a major problem. Here police officers in the city of Xi'an, China, burn confiscated illegal and fake guns during a campaign to destroy illegal weapons.*

Tougher Penalties

U.S. gun rights groups blame criminals for the rise in gun crime. They believe the best way to reduce it is to introduce tougher penalties for criminals. China's weapons laws are among the world's toughest. Private individuals are banned from owning rifles, pistols, and even gun replicas. Possession of a single gun can lead to a prison sentence as long as three years, and the penalty for a gun crime is often execution. In September 2007, a young man was found guilty of using a replica gun to rob a bank customer of $218,000 and was given a 19-year prison sentence. Yet a gun culture is still taking hold in China, and the police face increasingly well armed and aggressive criminals, so perhaps tough penalties are not the deterrent they appear to be.

FACT FILE

Maximum penalty for possession of an illegal weapon around the world:

- U.S. – varies; up to 10 years in prison
- UK – 10 years in prison
- Canada – 5 years in prison
- Mexico – 30 years in prison
- Japan – 10 years in prison and 1 million yen fine (around $12,000).

ARMING THE POLICE

How do you deal with armed criminals? Most police departments have special military-style units equipped with assault rifles, stun grenades, and even armored personnel carriers. By the time these special teams arrive on the scene, however, it may be too late; so in many departments all police officers carry guns.

Visible Security

Most countries in Europe and North America routinely arm police officers in the belief that guns are needed to protect the police and the public against a growing number of armed criminals. There is also the argument that people feel safer when they see armed police. For example, after the 9/11 terrorist attacks on New York, police officers at airports started carrying sub-machine guns. These would not necessarily make a big difference in an attack, but they are a lot more visible than pistols or other light arms.

BUSTED!

Not all countries generally arm their police officers. The United Kingdom, for example, only arms a special unit that deals with armed robbery. The unit stopped a high-profile robbery in 2000 when a gang tried to steal jewels worth over $553 million from the Millennium Dome, a London tourist attraction. The robbers planned to smash their way into the dome with a bulldozer and escape using a speedboat on the Thames River. The special unit disguised themselves as cleaners, hid their weapons, and quickly overpowered the gang members once they arrived.

► *South Africa has one of the highest violent crime rates in the world, so during the 2010 World Cup, the world's top soccer teams were escorted by armed police to and from the airports.*

Special Units

Almost every police department has special units that deal with armed criminals. Such units may prevent shoot-outs, as the threat of force is enough to make many armed gangs surrender. However, though these officers are highly trained, innocent people still get shot, either by mistake due to inaccurate information or because they get caught in the crossfire of a shoot-out. In March 2006, an unarmed doctor was shot and killed by a Special Weapons and Tactics (SWAT) team in Virginia. On July 22, 2005, a police anti-terrorist unit wrongly identified Brazilian Jean Charles De Menezes as a suicide bomber on the London subway system and killed him at close range. Many people were shocked that the British police had a shoot-to-kill policy.

Guns on the Beat

Most British police on the beat are not armed. The theory behind this is that once police officers have guns, they may be tempted to use their weapon rather than relying on less deadly options to stop a criminal, such as stun guns, tear gas, or simply talking them into surrendering. If police are not armed, some criminals may also choose not to arm themselves. They additionally know that using a weapon in a robbery will lead to a much tougher sentence if they are caught.

▼ *CCTV images captured the last movements of 27-year-old Brazilian Jean Charles de Menezes shortly before he was shot by anti-terrorist police at Stockwell subway station on July 22, 2005.*

WAR ON THE STREETS

The level of gang violence in developing countries such as Mexico and Brazil presents a new problem for governments and police departments. There's no easy way to fight powerful and heavily armed gangs, but using soldiers trained for the battlefield on crowded city streets inevitably leads to more deaths.

Slum Violence

In Brazil, 50,000 people are murdered each year. Many deaths occur in slums known as favelas. Many of these slums are controled by illegal armed groups, drug traffickers, or vigilante militias. Each week in the big Brazilian cities of São Paolo and Rio de Janeiro, the newspapers are filled with pictures of bulletproof vehicles and gun battles between drug gangs. In São Paolo, the police concentrate their attacks on drug gangs, while trying to improve the living conditions within the favelas. In Rio, however, the police battle gangs head-on—armed units go into the favelas with guns blazing, then occupy whole blocks for weeks or months. In 2009, around 1,000 people, including innocent bystanders, were killed in such police operations.

Trigger-Happy Police?

Brazil is not the only country where such extreme tactics are used. In Venezuela, police officers gun down an estimated 900 people every year. For every officer killed in a shoot-out, 39 suspects die. In Colombia during the early 2000s, "death squads" made up of off-duty soldiers and policemen patrolled the streets at night and gunned down thousands of government opponents each year.

▼ *Military officers keep watch on top of a slum house during an operation in the Rocinha favela in Rio de Janeiro, Brazil. In an attempt to stop bloody wars between rival drug gangs, the Brazilian police departments sometimes occupy such slums for many months.*

A War on Drugs

At the start of 2007, Mexican President Felipe Calderon declared war on drug traffickers, involving a force of around 45,000 troops and 5,000 police officers. So far, around 11,000 people have died, many in bloody shootouts and assassinations. Some were innocent bystanders who got caught in the crossfire. In the border city of Ciudad Juárez, police pickups and military trucks packed with heavily armed troops constantly patrol the streets. In February 2009, the city's police chief quit after several officers were killed and signs appeared threatening that more would be killed unless he stepped down. Three years into the war, it is far from won, and the bloodshed continues.

◄ *Felipe Calderon was elected President of Mexico in December 2006. He has vowed to take apart Mexico's powerful drug cartels as part of his election campaign.*

▼ *In 2008, police in Washington, D.C., attempted to tackle rising gun crime in the Trinidad neighborhood by creating a "Neighborhood Safety Zone." Police stopped cars at checkpoints on roads into the district. If drivers didn't have a good enough reason to be in the neighborhood, they were turned back.*

ON TARGET

In the neighborhood of Trinidad in Washington, D.C., police checkpoints have been used to control trouble hotspots following a rise in gun murders. This "occupation" style of policing follows methods developed by the Israeli police in Palestine. However, although roadblocks may make life difficult for armed criminals, they also make locals feel as if they are living in a police state where they are constantly being watched.

SOLVING GUN CRIME

Guns are deadly weapons, but they can also provide a trail of clues linking the victim, the weapon, and the shooter. Police officers arriving at the main crime scene interview witnesses and carefully record and collect every possible scrap of evidence. It is a long, complicated, and often tedious job—but one tiny bloodstain or fingerprint can solve the whole case.

At the Crime Scene

The main crime scene is where the shooting took place, though sometimes the victim's body or the gun are found elsewhere, and these also become crime scenes. Arriving at the scene, police officers will try to arrest the shooter and help any victims who are still alive. Their next job is to secure the crime scene. This means making sure that everything remains exactly the way it was when the crime happened.

The whole crime scene is then recorded with photos and sketches. Meanwhile, detectives take the names and addresses of witnesses and may ask them a few key questions, such as how many shots were fired. Finally, the crime scene investigators (CSIs) get down to the nitty-gritty of collecting evidence. They are very careful—if they're scraping a sample of blood from a window, for example, they must make sure they don't accidentally wipe off any fingerprints at the same time.

▲ *Forensics experts sift a crime scene looking for potential clues near the a river in England. They wear disposable jumpsuits to avoid contaminating the evidence.*

▲ *Although CCTV cameras can help investigators to track down criminals, hardened criminals can work their way around the surveillance by preventing the camera from getting a good shot of their face (in this case, the criminal is wearing a motorcycle helmet).*

Gathering Evidence

CCTV recording can provide valuable evidence to link a gunman to a crime scene. Police investigators can spend a long time looking through hours of CCTV footage back at the police station searching for the crucial image.

As well as looking for bullets, investigators at the scene look for used cartridge cases, which can show where the shooter stood. Markings on the bullet can confirm what weapon was used, while the angle at which it hits a wall indicates where the gun was fired from. All the evidence is sealed in plastic bags, and after being photographed or videotaped, it is sent to the crime lab.

ON TARGET

Though CCTV has great potential to detect gun crime, especially in banks and other enclosed spaces, one of its major drawbacks is that the operators often have to monitor many different cameras at once over long periods of time. At the moment, a new software program named MEDUSA is being developed that may help to detect someone carrying a gun or acting suspiciously. The software scans CCTV footage and looks for certain types of behaviors that suggest someone may be carrying a gun.

FIREARMS IN THE CRIME LAB

The first use of ballistics—figuring out the flight of a bullet—was by Joseph Bell, a 19th-century doctor who inspired the fictional detective Sherlock Holmes. In gun crimes today, firearms examiners spend most of their time peering through powerful microscopes at tiny dents and scratches on bullets and cartridges which tell them what kind of gun was used.

Key Evidence

At a crime scene, the victim's wounds, the bullets, and the gun are the key pieces of evidence. Fingerprints, blood splatters, and fibers from clothing can also link the gun user to the scene, the gun, or the victim. In a crime lab, forensic scientists test weapons and compare ammunition. Careful examination of bullets and cartridges with a microscope and a computer matching system, along with tests done on a firing range, will usually identify which weapon was used. The FBI lab in Los Angeles has a large collection of weapons that can be used for comparison.

Comparing Firearms

Gun records can give the background to a weapon recovered by the police. At the FBI, the Firearms-Toolmarks Unit examines firearms, toolmarks, and ammunition found at a crime scene. The people in this unit examine bullets to try to match them to a gun. If they suspect a certain gun of being used in the crime, they can compare the bullets directly. Otherwise, they can use a national database of bullets to try to find a match.

▼ *Many forensic scientists specialize in one area, such as firearms, blood splatters, or fingerprints. Despite what you see on TV, forensic scientists don't interview anyone—they leave that to the detectives.*

▲ *A firearms officer discharges a pistol in a crime lab in Los Angeles, California. Every gun leaves trademark marks and scratches on a bullet.*

Telltale Signs

Lab technicians test a weapon for all sorts of clues to see if they match up with witness statements.

- To see if it may go off accidentally, if this is part of the shooter's defense.
- The spread of gunshot residue can show if someone was shot at very close range, often a sign of a gang shooting rather than someone shooting in self-defense.
- If there is no gunshot residue on the victim's hands, it proves it was not a suicide and that the gun may have been planted in his or her hand after the shooting.
- Taking a weapon apart may also show if it has been converted from a fake into a real weapon.

ON TARGET

A new law in California means that every semi-automatic handgun sold in the state will "microstamp" each bullet cartridge in two places whenever it is fired. The stamp would identify the gun's make, model, and serial number.

CASE STUDY: THE WASHINGTON SNIPER

On October 3, 2002, an unknown gunman shot and killed five people in 15 hours in a suburb of Washington, D.C. The next day the shootings continued, and a massive police operation was launched. Tracking down the killer was going to take a combination of good detective skills, forensics—and luck.

Fear and Panic

A wave of fear quickly spread through the local community, mainly because there seemed no logic to the attacks. The first victim was shot in a grocery store parking lot, while others were shot mowing the lawn, filling a car with gas, or sitting on a bench. A few days later, a 13-year-old boy was shot outside his school. Though eyewitness accounts of the killings were confused, the evidence showed that most of the victims had been shot from long range, and the killer quickly became known as the "Washington Sniper."

Message from a Killer

The sniper began taunting the police with cryptic messages. He left tarot cards at several crime scenes, one with the message "Dear Mr Police. Code: Call me God." Later, the killer left handwritten notes demanding $10 million. One ended with the chilling message: "Your children are not safe anywhere or anytime." As more people were shot, the police desperately searched for a clue that would help them track down the killer.

▼ *Police officers prepare to search the parking lot where the sniper's 10th victim, FBI Intelligence Officer Linda Franklin, was found.*

The Breakthrough

The sniper called the police and boasted of a previous attack in the town of Montgomery, Alabama. Police traced the call and rushed to the pay phone, but they missed the killer by just a few minutes. However, on October 17, they discovered that a fingerprint found at a previous shooting in Montgomery matched one found near the school in Washington where the 13-year-old boy had been murdered. The print belonged to a 17-year-old man named Lee Malvo.

Capture

Further detective work linked Malvo with another man named John Allen Muhammed, the owner of a blue Chevrolet Caprice. Witnesses had reported seeing this car near several of the shootings. Finally, on October 24, after the media informed the public about the Caprice, it was spotted in a highway rest area in the state of Maryland. The police found Malvo and Muhammed sleeping inside, along with a high-powered rifle. The police later matched the rifle to 11 of the 14 bullets found at earlier crime scenes. Muhammed was later found guilty of mass murder and executed on November 10, 2009. Malvo was sentenced to life in prison for his role in the killings.

▼ *Police officers bring suspect Lee Malvo into court during the trial of sniper John Allen Muhammad.*

ON TARGET

The police realized they might have caught the two gunmen sooner if they had been able to match the sniper's bullets to those taken from the crime scene of the shooting in Montgomery. After the trial, a national database was set up to help local police departments match bullets with those in other states. Digital images allow bullets found at a crime scene to be matched to others in a few hours.

TACKLING GUN CRIME

Tighter gun control, better detective work, and harsher prison sentences are all suggested as ways of tackling gun crime. Others argue that it can only be tackled effectively by dealing with the broader issues behind it, such as poverty and drug abuse. While some violent criminals do have extreme personalities, many others are drawn into the gun culture by a lack of opportunity or education.

Guns and Drugs

Gun crimes are often committed by criminal gangs with links to the drug trade. Enormous profits can be made quickly, and gangs arm themselves to protect their empires. A feud between rival drug gangs can soon turn into an arms race.

Police gang raids have uncovered weapons such as assault rifles, machine guns, and grenade launchers. While there is so much money to be made from drugs, tighter gun control and increased prison sentences are unlikely to have any effect. Such gun crimes may only be stopped when it is no longer so profitable to deal in drugs.

▼ *The Crips and Bloods gangs based in many U.S. cities are bitter enemies, often leading to open and bloody warfare on the streets. These gang members show their allegiance to the Bloods by wearing red (the Crips wear blue).*

▲ *In Los Angeles, the annual Gun Buyback program encourages gun owners to exchange weapons for a grocery store gift card or a prepaid credit card. About 2,500 firearms were collected in 2010.*

Community Projects

In the United States, Project Safe Neighborhoods (PSN) aims to reduce gun and gang crime by funding local programs that provide training, hand out gun lock safety kits, and help to prevent troubled teenagers from getting drawn into the gun culture. The program recognizes the fact that the reasons for gun crime often vary in different places, and a local approach works better to prevent gun crime.

Firearms Amnesty

Governments all over the world have tried to reduce the number of guns in their country with a firearms amnesty. In China, for instance, posters in subways ask people to hand in weapons to a local police station with no questions asked, or even for cash. A six-month campaign in 2008 led to 79,000 guns, 1.8 million replicas, and 5.75 million bullets being handed in.

ON TARGET

The British anti-gun crime charity the Disarm Trust was set up after two teenage girls were killed in Birmingham, England in 2003 during New Year celebrations. The trust works with local community groups in poor neighborhoods where many young people have limited education and few job opportunities. They want to break the cycle of older criminals leading younger people into a life of crime and prevent the spread of guns. The government helped to set up the charity using money recovered from convicted criminals.

CASE STUDY: OPERATION TRIDENT

Operation Trident is an anti-gun operation set up to help bring an end to a series of shootings and murders among young black people in London. It aims to tackle gun crime by working with community leaders and running high profile advertising campaigns aimed at encouraging young people to break away from the gun culture.

Police Initiatives

Operation Trident was launched in July 2000 to deal with violent crimes in London's black community, partly caused by the spread of the drug and turf wars between rival Jamaican, African, and British-born gangs. The rise in gun crime in London has also been caused by easier access to weapons. A growing number of teenagers not linked to gangs have gotten involved in "respect shootings" to settle petty arguments. There is an automatic 30-year prison sentence for murder, so a recent tactic has been to shoot victims in the leg to avoid killing them.

Vital Evidence

Intelligence gathering is a very important part of the operation, but it is not easy, as many gangs are divided into smaller units, each with their own names. As gang members have often known each other since they were students, it is also difficult to infiltrate them. Trident's campaigns encourage people to call with information relating to gun crime. These ads appear in newspapers, in nightclubs, on gas pumps, and on the radio. One ad pointed out the dangers of carrying toy or imitation guns, while others highlight the brutal—and deadly—consequences of gun crime. However, even if people do call with good information, it can be

► This ad was designed by Operation Trident. It uses the simple children's game "rock-paper-scissors" to encourage members of London's black community to call with information about gun crime.

very hard to get witnesses to appear in court and testify. Critics of Trident say this is because there is not enough police protection, and witnesses are too afraid of what will happen to them or their families if they give evidence.

The Reality of Gun Crime

Operation Trident recognizes that poor job opportunities make it easy for drug gangs to tempt young people into crime by offering them large sums of money. It organizes anti-gun talks for elementary school children and teenagers, and the speakers are often ex-criminals who don't want others to make the same mistakes they did. One explains to the audience the grim reality of spending 20 years in prison: "No play stations, no Nintendo, hardcore jail where you've got someone telling you what to do, where to go, when to take a shower, and when to go to bed."

BUSTED!

In June 2008, Operation Trident investigated the murder of 15-year-old Michael Dosunmu. The evidence given by six witnesses was key to the case. To protect their identities, the witnesses were hidden behind screens, and three had their voices changed by computer technology so they could not be recognized. When witnesses don't come forward, technology and painstaking detective work can help. In March 2005, two young men were convicted of the murder of Letisha Shakespeare and Charlene Ellis. The women were killed outside a hair salon in Birmingham, England in 2003, and police found their killers thanks to detailed cell phone evidence that tied them to the scene.

▼ Wayne Rowe (far right) is one of several reformed gang members who now work for Operation Trident. He talks to young people about the grim reality of gun crime and his experiences in prison.

GUN CRIME IN THE MEDIA

Many argue that the media is a bad influence on people's attitudes toward guns and gun crime. Movies often feature guns and shoot-outs, glamorizing guns and making extreme violence seem normal. Meanwhile, news reports of murders and other violent crimes can make ordinary people afraid, even though their chances of being affected by gun crime are relatively slim.

A Powerful Allure

Movies, TV shows, and violent computer games help to glorify the gun—the gunman is often made to look cool or in control, while carrying a gun is made to seem the most natural thing in the world. As a result, guns have a powerful appeal, even if they are never used. Gang members often wear them as a symbol of their deadly power and revel in the fear they inspire in their victims and enemies.

Is There a Link?

In some police shows, shots are fired in every other scene and deaths are common. By the time average American children reach the age of 18, they have witnessed 16,000 murders and 200,000 acts of violence on screen. However, after 50 years and hundreds of different studies, scientists cannot agree whether there is a direct link between violence on screen and violence in real life. Though TV shows can make violence seem normal and do make some children more aggressive, there are many other reasons why violent crimes are committed.

▼ *James Bond, licensed to kill. Movies and TV shows have long glamorized guns, but the reality of gun crime is brutal, shocking, and tragic.*

▲ *One of the criticisms of video games is that they make people more violent. But most studies show this is only true when that person is naturally aggressive or is having other problems at home or in school.*

BUSTED!

Rap music with violent and aggressive language has also been blamed for encouraging gun crime and glamorizing gangs. In its defense, some argue that movies and computer games glorify guns far more than music, and there are more important causes of violent crime. However, rap's violent image wasn't helped when hip-hop star T.I. was convicted in May 2009 after FBI agents found his car contained several machine guns and his jacket was stuffed with bullets. They also discovered a weapons store at his home, including a laser-sighted sniper rifle.

Gun Crime in the News

Real-life crime stories grab people's attention and sell newspapers. Violent crimes, especially murders, often get a lot of coverage. As a result of this, it sometimes seems that gun crime is a lot more prevalent than it really is. Some journalists argue that reporting murders is important, as it reinforces the point that killing is wrong and shocking. Others argue that there is demand from the public to feature crime stories. But along with this interest comes the element of fear, which can encourage people to own a weapon to defend themselves. Ironically, those least likely to be victims of crime are those most likely to be afraid—the elderly—while those most at risk—young men—are least likely to worry.

► *Hip-hop stars such as NWA, Snoop Dogg, and T.I. (right) have been criticized for glamorizing guns in their lyrics. They claim they are just reflecting real life on the streets.*

AN ONGOING DEBATE

The debate over gun laws remains a hot topic in many countries. While some politicians campaign for tighter controls, gun enthusiasts refuse to give up their arms. As a result, gun control laws vary wildly even within one country. In U.S. cities such as New York or Chicago, it is difficult or impossible to legally keep guns for self-defense, while in other parts of the country, the gun laws are very relaxed.

◄ *Guns are deadly. When they get into the wrong hands, the outcome can be devastating. Australian Martin John Bryant murdered 35 people and injured 21 after he went on a shooting spree in Port Arthur, Tasmania in 1996.*

ON TARGET

Some experts argue that gun manufacturers should be forced to adopt "smart gun" technology to help prevent gun crime. In the future, all guns could be computerized with special sensors that would prevent anyone except the owner of the gun from using it.

Variations in the Law

Some countries are creating tighter gun controls. Australia, for example, introduced new laws after the Port Arthur massacre in 1996 in which 35 people died. There has also been a campaign in Australia by police and shooting organizations to encourage gun owners to make sure their weapons are kept under lock and key. This has led to a big reduction in the number of stolen weapons. In the United Kingdom, anyone caught carrying a replica gun in public gets an automatic five-year jail sentence. Meanwhile, some states in the United States have been heading in the opposite direction. In 2005, Florida introduced a law allowing citizens the right to "stand their ground" and open fire even in a public place if they feel threatened.

Working with Gun Owners

Some argue, however, that it's almost impossible to outlaw guns—there are just too many of them around already. They want the police to work with gun clubs to clamp down on the black market for weapons, which supplies many of the criminal gangs. Gun enthusiasts are often aware of the gun shops that will sell to anyone. The Boston Gun Project has been very successful in tackling gun crime by targeting dealers who sold guns that ended up in the hands of criminals.

What's the Future?

Gun crime remains a problem for many countries. In the United Kingdom, after many years without mass shootings, a shooting spree by taxi driver Derrick Bird in June 2010 reopened the gun laws debate. Despite the arguments, few would disagree that new ways need to be found to prevent gun crime, whether by gun control, better detective methods, working with local communities, or dealing with the bigger related issues such as drugs and poverty.

▲ *British police officers do not routinely carry guns, and they are some of the few in the world who follow this practice. But the rise of violent crime in London and the threat from terrorists has led to more armed police officers on the city's streets.*

ON TARGET

Police and law enforcement agencies have teamed up in a new anti-gun crime program in the city of Minneapolis after the homicide rate there rose dramatically in 2010. The plan will add longer sentences for criminals who use and sell guns. In particular, the team hopes to clamp down on people who buy guns and then sell them to criminals.

GLOSSARY

assassin a murderer who targets particular victims, often important people, and kills them in a surprise attack; assassins are often paid to kill.

automatic weapon a gun that reloads itself and keeps firing until the trigger is released

ballistics the study of flying bullets

black market buying something, such as a gun, from an illegal source

bulletproof describes something, such as a car window or door, that is strong enough to stop a bullet

bystander someone who is at a crime scene but who does not take part; bystanders are often important witnesses, and they can also get hit in gun battles between the police and criminals.

CCTV closed-circuit television; a system that uses video cameras to watch a particular place, such as banks, airports, and jewelry stores

DNA (deoxyribonucleic acid) the main molecule that holds genetic information in living things

drug cartel an organization that controls the production, supply, and sale of illegal drugs

FBI (Federal Bureau of Investigation) U.S. government security service responsible for solving crimes

firearm a gun such as a handgun, shotgun, or rifle

forensics scientific tests or techniques used to investigate crimes

gun control laws created to control the sale of guns

gun culture how guns are used in society; it is much more common to own a gun in some countries than in others.

gun rights groups groups that believe people have a right to own or carry guns

gun shows an exhibition where firearms and ammunition are bought and sold

handgun a firearm with a short barrel usually used with one hand, such as a pistol or revolver

homicide a murder or illegal death caused by another person

killing spree when a murderer kills two or more victims in a short span of time

licence a permit, for example to own a gun

machine gun a rapidly firing automatic weapon

massacre when lots of people are killed at the same time, usually in a violent way

militia people who have trained as soldiers but are not part of a regular army

reasonable force also called legal force; the amount of force a person or police officer can use to protect themselves while staying within the law

replica a copy; replica guns are sometimes used by criminals in a robbery and can also be adapted to fire real bullets.

rifle a long-barrelled gun that fires bullets; the grooves or rifling along its barrel help the bullet to travel in a straight line, and it is designed for use at long range.

semiautomatic a firearm that fires a single shot and reloads each time the trigger is pulled

serial killer someone who murders more than three victims in separate incidents in a short span of time

shoot-to-kill a policy of killing dangerous suspects without trying to arrest or question them

shotgun a gun with a long smooth barrel that fires shot (small metal balls)

sniper a marksman who shoots at people from a concealed place, often at long range

tear gas a gas used by police to control riots or violent suspects; effects include tears streaming from the eyes, coughing, dizziness, and vomiting.

trafficker someone who smuggles illegal goods, especially drugs or guns

vigilante someone who takes the law into their own hands; vigilantes punish criminals themselves rather than going to the police.

FURTHER INFORMATION

Books

Cooper, Chris. *Forensic Science (Eyewitness Books),* DK Publishing, 2008.

Lankford, Ronnie ed. *Gun Violence (Social Issues Firsthand),* Greenhaven Press, 2010.

Royston, Angela. *Gun Crimes (Solve It With Science),* Smart Apple Media, 2010.

Web Sites

www.fbi.gov/fbikids.htm
The kids section of the Federal Bureau of Investigation web site allows young people to learn more about the FBI through games, stories, and interactives. It also shows how FBI agents and analysts investigate serious crimes.

www.atf.gov/firearms/enforcement/
This is the site of the Bureau of Alcohol, Tobacco, Firearms, and Explosives, which regulates gun licensing in the United States.

www.ncjrs.gov/App/Topics/Topic.aspx?topicid=87
Administered by the U.S. Department of Justice, this is the National Criminal Justice Reference Service's web site, which publishes reports and statistics on gun violence.

www.jhsph.edu/gunpolicy
Part of Johns Hopkins University, the Center for Gun Policy and Research is an organization dedicated to reducing gun violence using research and public health principles.

www.psn.gov/default.aspx
Project Safe Neighborhoods, sponsored by the U.S. Department of Justice, is an organization that seeks to reduce gun and gang crime by providing resources to local programs.

Note to parents and teachers: Every effort has been made by the publishers to ensure that these web sites are suitable for children, that they are of the highest educational value, and that they contain no inappropriate or offensive material. However, because of the nature of the Internet, it is impossible to guarantee that the contents of these sites will not be altered. We strongly advise that Internet access is supervised by a responsible adult.

INDEX

SERIES CONTENTS

Cybercrime Inside Picture • Hacking • Case Study: Gary McKinnon • Phishing • Cyberbullying • Cyberstalking • Virus Attacks • Malware • Social Networking Sites • Fraudulent Web Sites • Denial-of-Service Attacks • Identity Theft • Case Study: Pirate Bay • Cyberterrorism • Cyber Wars • Case Study: Cyber Wars in Eastern Europe • Cybersecurity

Drug Crime Drug Crime: A Worldwide Problem • Which Drugs Are Illegal? • Who Are the Criminals? • The Flow of Drugs • The Cost of Drugs • Tackling the Traffickers • Smuggling and Mules • Case Study: Below the Waves! • Stop and Search • Global Drug Watch • Surveillance • Case Study: Operation Junglefowl • Going Undercover • The Bust • Case Study: Operation Habitat • Rehabilitation • The Future

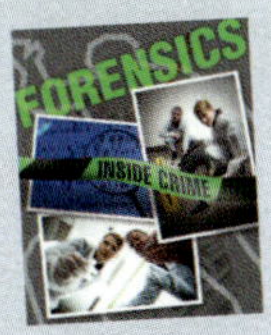

Forensics Inside Picture • Fingerprinting • Securing the Crime Scene • The Autopsy • Natural Clues: Insects • Soils and Seeds • Using Blood • DNA Evidence • Bones and Skulls • Case Study: The Body Farm • Clothes and Shoes • Paper Trail • Guns and Bullets • Drugs and Poisons • Crash Investigations • Fire Investigations • Case Study: Lockerbie Bombing

Gun Crime Gun Crime—Out of Control? • What Is Gun Crime? • What Guns Are Used? • Who Commits Gun Crimes? • Case Study: Killing Sprees • How Much Gun Crime Is There? • Getting Hold of Guns • Controls and Penalties • Arming the Police • War on the Streets • Solving Gun Crime • Firearms in the Crime Lab • Case Study: The Washington Sniper • Tackling Gun Crime • Case Study: Operation Trident • Gun Crime in the Media • An Ongoing Debate

Juvenile Crime Inside Picture • Changing Times • Cracking Down on Kids • Everybody Does It! • The Problem with Sex • The Alcohol Demon • Drugs and Young People • Gangs • Case Study: Youth Gangs in South Africa • Armed and Dangerous • Children Who Kill • Case Study: The Story of Mary Bell • School and College Massacres • On Trial • Locked Up • Alternatives to Prison • Prevention Is Better Than Cure

Kidnapping and Piracy Inside Picture • In the Past • Piracy at Sea • Somalia • Case Study: MV Sirius Star • Policing the Pirates • Prosecution and Detention • Kidnapping for Ransom • Abducting Children • Taken Hostage • Case Study: Lebanon • Hijacking • Case Study: 9/11 • Negotiation • Armed Response • Training and Support • Surviving a Kidnapping

People Trafficking Inside Picture • How Did We Get Here? • The Traffickers • The Victims • Forced Labor • The Sex Industry • Trafficking Children • Source Countries • In Transit • Border Controls • Case Study: The European Union • Caught in the Act • Loopholes in the Law • Police and Welfare • Working with NGOs • Raising Awareness • Taking a Stand

Policing and Justice What Is Criminal Justice? • Rough Justice • Enforcing the Law • Dealing with Serious Crimes • Officers of the Law • Case Study: Racism by the Police • Guarding the Guardians • Case Study: Reforming the Police • The Criminal Justice System • Arrest and Detention • Seeking Justice: The Courts • Punishment • Alternatives to Prison • Juvenile Justice • Case Study: Dealing with Terrorism • Victims' Rights • The Future